ANOINTING 101

ANOINTING 101

ANOINTING FOR THE NEW MILLENNIUM.

© 1999 Matthew Ashimolowo
Published by Mattyson Media an imprint of MAMM

Matthew Ashimolowo Media Ministries
57 Waterden Road
Hackney Wick
London
E15 2EE

All rights reserved. No part of this publication may be reproduced, stored in a retrieval system, or be transmitted, in any form, or by any means, mechanical, electronic, photocopying or otherwise without prior written consent of the publisher.

Bible quotes are from the King James Bible unless otherwise stated.

ISBN 1 874646-27-9

ANOINTING 101

WHAT
&
WHY

ANOINTING 101

The anointing is the reward of the Holy Spirit for commitment and pursuit of Him.

"And ye shall seek me, and find me, when ye shall search for me with all your heart." Jeremiah 29: 13

You were programmed for wonders.

"Behold, I and the children whom the LORD hath given me are for signs and for wonders in Israel from the LORD of hosts, which dwelleth in mount Zion." Isaiah 8:18

ANOINTING 101

The anointing helps you see events occurring in the world.

"Call to Me and I will answer you and show you great and mighty things, fenced in and hidden, which you do not know (do not distinguish and recognise, have knowledge of and understand)." Jeremiah 33: 3 (Amplied)

The anointing is the Holy Presence and Power of God.

"But ye have an unction from the Holy One, and ye know all things."
1 John 2: 20

"But the anointing which ye have received of him abideth in you, and ye need not that any man teach you: but as the same anointing teacheth you of all things, and is truth, and is no lie, and even as it hath taught you, ye shall abide in him." 1 John 2: 27

The anointing forces a decision.

"Now when they saw the boldness of Peter and John, and perceived that they were unlearned and ignorant men, they marvelled; and they took knowledge of them, that they had been with Jesus. And beholding the man which was healed standing with them, they could say nothing against it."
Acts 4: 13-14

The anointing uses the word as a force that demands a response.

"For the word of God is quick, and powerful, and sharper than any two-edged sword, piercing even to the dividing asunder of soul and spirit, and of the joints and marrow, and is a discerner of the thoughts and intents of the heart. Neither is there any creature that is not manifest in his sight: but all things are naked and opened unto the eyes of him with whom we have to do." Hebrews 4:12-13

ANOINTING 101

The anointing consecrates, imparts holiness and power.

"And thou shalt sanctify them, that they may be most holy: whatsoever toucheth them shall be holy." Exodus 30:29

ANOINTING 101

The anointing is your key to winning.

"Then he answered and spake unto me, saying, This is the word of the LORD unto Zerubbabel, saying, Not by might, nor by power, but by my spirit, saith the LORD of hosts." Zechariah 4:6

ANOINTING 101

It's senseless trying not to use the power in you.

"Wherefore I put thee in remembrance that thou stir up the gift of God, which is in thee by the putting on of my hands." 2 Timothy 1: 6

ANOINTING 101

When you have the anointing, you have the strength no force can overcome.

"But my horn shalt thou exalt like the horn of an unicorn: I shall be anointed with fresh oil. Mine eye also shall see my desire on mine enemies, and mine ears shall hear my desire of the wicked that rise up against me."
Psalm 92:10-11

ANOINTING 101

An anointed person is a danger to satan.

"He that committeth sin is of the devil; for the devil sinneth from the beginning. For this purpose the Son of God was manifested, that he might destroy the works of the devil." 1 John 3:8

ANOINTING 101

Evil turns on the planner when you are anointed.

"Saying, Touch not mine anointed, and do my prophets no harm." Psalm 105:15

ANOINTING 101

The Anointing makes you go where others dread.

"As they ministered to the Lord, and fasted, the Holy Ghost said, Separate me Barnabas and Saul for the work whereunto I have called them. And when they had fasted and prayed, and laid their hands on them, they sent them away. So they, being sent forth by the Holy Ghost, departed unto Seleucia; and from thence they sailed to Cyprus. Acts 13: 2-4

ANOINTING 101

Anointed one means the one that was empowered to accomplish.

"I can do all things through Christ which strengtheneth me."   *Philippians 4:13*

There is a mystery about the anointed one.

"How God anointed Jesus of Nazareth with the Holy Ghost and with power: who went about doing good, and healing all that were oppressed of the devil; for God was with him." Acts 10:38

"Withal praying also for us, that God would open unto us a door of utterance, to speak the mystery of Christ, for which I am also in bonds."
Colossians 4: 3

ANOINTING 101

You cannot understand Jesus until you understand the anointing.

"How God anointed Jesus of Nazareth with the Holy Ghost and with power: who went about doing good, and healing all that were oppressed of the devil; for God was with him." Acts 10:38

ANOINTING 101

The anointing is the force behind sweat-less victory.

"Now the Lord is that Spirit: and where the Spirit of the Lord is, there is liberty." 2 Corinthians 3:17

"Then he answered and spake unto me, saying, This is the word of the LORD unto Zerubbabel, saying, Not by might, nor by power, but by my spirit, saith the LORD of hosts." Zechariah 4: 6

ANOINTING 101

The level of your anointing determines your productivity.

"Thou lovest righteousness, and hatest wickedness: therefore God, thy God, hath anointed thee with the oil of gladness above thy fellows." Psalm 45:7

ANOINTING 101

You cannot occupy your rightful place without the anointing.

"Then Peter said, Silver and gold have I none; but such as I have give I thee: In the name of Jesus Christ of Nazareth rise up and walk." Acts 3:6

ANOINTING 101

There is deliverance in anointed praise, worship and message.

"And at midnight Paul and Silas prayed, and sang praises unto God: and the prisoners heard them. And suddenly there was a great earthquake, so that the foundations of the prison were shaken: and immediately all the doors were opened, and every one's bands were loosed." Acts 16:25-26

ANOINTING 101

Anointed preachers, singers, and churches are known if the burden is removed and the yoke is destroyed.

"Then upon Jahaziel the son of Zechariah, the son of Benaiah, the son of Jeiel, the son of Mattaniah, a Levite of the sons of Asaph, came the Spirit of the LORD in the midst of the congregation;" 2 Chronicles 20:14

ANOINTING 101

The clue to an anointed wife or husband is the removal of burdens.

"And Isaac brought her into his mother Sarah's tent, and took Rebekah, and she became his wife; and he loved her: and Isaac was comforted after his mother's death." Genesis 24:67

ANOINTING 101

The anointing does not just break but destroy the yoke.

"And it shall come to pass in that day, that his burden shall be taken away from off thy shoulder, and his yoke from off thy neck, and the yoke shall be destroyed because of the anointing." Isaiah 10:27

Nothing works without the anointing.

"Howbeit this kind goeth not out but by prayer and fasting."
Matthew 17:21

ANOINTING 101

The level to which it flows to you is to the degree that you honour your man or woman of God.

"Render therefore to all their dues: tribute to whom tribute is due; custom to whom custom; fear to whom fear; honor to whom honor." Romans 13: 7

ANOINTING 101

The anointing makes you to be immune from poisons and live in divine protection, where nothing of the enemy can harm or destroy us.

"They shall take up serpents; and if they drink any deadly thing, it shall not hurt them; they shall lay hands on the sick, and they shall recover."
Mark 16:18

ANOINTING 101

The anointing is given to execute judgement upon God's enemies by the power of the Holy Spirit.

"But Peter said, Ananias, why hath Satan filled thine heart to lie to the Holy Ghost, and to keep back part of the price of the land? Whiles it remained, was it not thine own? and after it was sold, was it not in thine own power? why hast thou conceived this thing in thine heart? thou hast not lied unto men, but unto God. And Ananias hearing these words fell down, and gave up the ghost: and great fear came on all them that heard these things."

Acts 5:3-5

ANOINTING 101

To impart the baptism of the Holy Spirit to other believers.

"Then laid they their hands on them, and they received the Holy Ghost."
Acts 8:17

To exercise all nine gifts of the Spirit.

"But the manifestation of the Spirit is given to every man to profit withal. For to one is given by the Spirit the word of wisdom; to another the word of knowledge by the same Spirit; To another faith by the same Spirit; to another the gifts of healing by the same Spirit; To another the working of miracles; to another prophecy; to another discerning of spirits; to another divers kinds of tongues; to another the interpretation of tongues: But all these worketh that one and the selfsame Spirit, dividing to every man severally as he will." 1 Corinthians 12:7-11

ANOINTING 101

To impart spiritual gifts to other believers.

"For I long to see you, that I may impart unto you some spiritual gift, to the end ye may be established." Romans 1:11

ANOINTING 101

To bind and loose and exercise authority, in the name of Jesus, over all the works of the devil.

"Verily I say unto you, Whatsoever ye shall bind on earth shall be bound in heaven: and whatsoever ye shall loose on earth shall be loosed in heaven."
Matthew 18:18

ANOINTING 101

To receive supernatural guidance, instruction and direction from the Holy Spirit.

"As they ministered to the Lord, and fasted, the Holy Ghost said, Separate me Barnabas and Saul for the work whereunto I have called them."
Acts 13:2

ANOINTING 101

To carry the presence and anointing of God and manifest all kinds of miracles, signs and wonders.

"God also bearing them witness, both with signs and wonders, and with divers miracles, and gifts of the Holy Ghost, according to his own will?"
Hebrews 2:4

ANOINTING 101

To walk in complete freedom from the bondage of sickness, poverty, false doctrines and demon powers.

"Stand fast therefore in the liberty wherewith Christ hath made us free, and be not entangled again with the yoke of bondage." Galatians 5:1

ANOINTING 101

To preach the uncompromised word of God with power and boldness.

"And when they had prayed, the place was shaken where they were assembled together; and they were all filled with the Holy Ghost, and they spake the word of God with boldness." Acts 4:31

ANOINTING 101

To have the power of God to do all things, where nothing is impossible.

"Jesus said unto him, If thou canst believe, all things are possible to him that believeth." Mark 9:23

ANOINTING 101

To cast out demons and heal the sick of all kinds of diseases.

"Then he called his twelve disciples together, and gave them power and authority over all devils, and to cure diseases. And he sent them to preach the kingdom of God, and to heal the sick." Luke 9:1-2

To cleanse the lepers and incurable diseases.

"Heal the sick, cleanse the lepers, raise the dead, cast out devils: freely ye have received, freely give." Matthew 10:8

ANOINTING 101

To raise the dead and get all prayers answered.

"If ye abide in me, and my words abide in you, ye shall ask what ye will, and it shall be done unto you." John 15:7

ANOINTING 101

To exercise power over all the power of the devil and destroy the works of the devil.

"Behold, I give unto you power to tread on serpents and scorpions, and over all the power of the enemy: and nothing shall by any means hurt you."
Luke 10:19

"Submit yourselves therefore to God. Resist the devil, and he will flee from you." James 4:7

ANOINTING 101

To do works as great and even greater than Jesus did.

"Verily, verily, I say unto you, He that believeth on me, the works that I do shall he do also; and greater works than these shall he do; because I go unto my Father." John 14:12

ANOINTING 101

To proclaim the good news to the poor.

"The Spirit of the Lord is upon me, because he hath anointed me to preach the gospel to the poor; he hath sent me to heal the brokenhearted, to preach deliverance to the captives, and recovering of sight to the blind, to set at liberty them that are bruised." Luke 4:18

ANOINTING 101

To set the captives free by the anointing of God.

"And they cast out many devils, and anointed with oil many that were sick, and healed them." Mark 6:13

To restore sight to the blind.

"And in that same hour he cured many of their infirmities and plagues, and of evil spirits; and unto many that were blind he gave sight."
Luke 7:21

ANOINTING 101

To restore hearing to the deaf.

"The blind receive their sight, and the lame walk, the lepers are cleansed, and the deaf hear, the dead are raised up, and the poor have the gospel preached to them." Matthew 11:5

ANOINTING 101

To cause cripples to walk and the lame to be made whole.

"And there sat a certain man at Lystra, impotent in his feet, being a cripple from his mother's womb, who never had walked: The same heard Paul speak: who steadfastly beholding him, and perceiving that he had faith to be healed, Said with a loud voice, Stand upright on thy feet. And he leaped and walked." Acts 14:8-10

ANOINTING 101

It is the key to changing your ministry from causing death to imparting life.

"Dead flies cause the ointment of the apothecary to send forth a stinking savor: so doth a little folly him that is in reputation for wisdom and honor."
Ecclesiastes 10:1

HOW TO HAVE IT

ANOINTING 101

Keep your motives consistent with God's.

"And when Simon saw that through laying on of the apostles' hands the Holy Ghost was given, he offered them money, Saying, Give me also this power, that on whomsoever I lay hands, he may receive the Holy Ghost. But Peter said unto him, Thy money perish with thee, because thou hast thought that the gift of God may be purchased with money." Acts 8:18-20

ANOINTING 101

Change your prayer life.

"The LORD is nigh unto all them that call upon him, to all that call upon him in truth." Psalm 145:18

ANOINTING 101

Get re-filled everyday.

"And be not drunk with wine, wherein is excess; but be filled with the Spirit; Speaking to yourselves in psalms and hymns and spiritual songs, singing and making melody in your heart to the Lord; Giving thanks always for all things unto God and the Father in the name of our Lord Jesus Christ."
Ephesians 5:18-20

ANOINTING 101

Learn to yield to the Holy Spirit.

"Know ye not, that to whom ye yield yourselves servants to obey, his servants ye are to whom ye obey; whether of sin unto death, or of obedience unto righteousness?" Romans 6: 16

Fellowship with the Holy Spirit.

"The grace of the Lord Jesus Christ, and the love of God, and the communion of the Holy Ghost, be with you all. Amen."
2 Corinthians 13:14

Be consistent.

- Crave the power of God daily.
- The furnace of passage for those who would be pure gold.

ANOINTING 101

- ### Take up the rod and do signs.

> "And I, behold, I will harden the hearts of the Egyptians, and they shall follow them: and I will get me honor upon Pharaoh, and upon all his host, upon his chariots, and upon his horsemen." Exodus 14:17

- ### Faith proclamation precedes possession.

- ### The sacrifice of cultivation is what determines a successful farmer.

ANOINTING 101

16 KEYS TO THE ANOINTING

Deep Spiritual Hunger

"Blessed are they which do hunger and thirst after righteousness: for they shall be filled." Matthew 5:6

- **For more of God.**

- **To see burdens removed and yokes destroyed.**

Prayer Power

> **More power is released as the believer prays.**

"But ye, beloved, building up yourselves on your most holy faith, praying in the Holy Ghost." Jude 20

"And they were all filled with the Holy Ghost, and began to speak with other tongues, as the Spirit gave them utterance." Acts 2:4

Exercising your Faith.

"But without faith it is impossible to please him: for he that cometh to God must believe that he is, and that he is a rewarder of the that diligently seek him." Hebrews 11: 6

ANOINTING 101

Acting on the Word of God.

"For with God nothing shall be impossible." Luke 1:37

"And they went forth, and preached every where, the Lord working with them, and confirming the word with signs following. Amen." Mark 16:20

ANOINTING 101

Dependence on the name of Jesus.

"And his name through faith in his name hath made this man strong, whom ye see and know: yea, the faith which is by him hath given him this perfect soundness in the presence of you all." Acts 3:16

ANOINTING 101

Genuine desire to help people.

- **You move in the anointing when you are compassionate.**

- **The anointing flows where there is love**

"And Jesus went forth, and saw a great multitude, and was moved with compassion toward them, and he healed their sick." Matthew 14:14

ANOINTING 101

The anointing is released when you act in faith.

"And these signs shall follow them that believe; In my name shall they cast out devils; they shall speak with new tongues; They shall take up serpents; and if they drink any deadly thing, it shall not hurt them; they shall lay hands on the sick, and they shall recover." Mark 16:17-18

ANOINTING 101

Making a demand on the anointing when present.

"For she said, If I may touch but his clothes, I shall be whole. And straightway the fountain of her blood was dried up; and she felt in her body that she was healed of that plague." Mark 5:28-29

Keep your motives consistent with God's.

"And when Simon saw that through laying on of the apostles' hands the Holy Ghost was given, he offered them money. Saying, Give me also this power, that on whomsoever I lay hands, he may receive the Holy Ghost. But Peter said unto him, Thy money perish with thee, because thou hast thought that the gift of God may be purchased with money. Thou hast neither part nor lot in this matter: for thy heart is not right in the sight of God. Repent therefore of this thy wickedness, and pray God, if perhaps the thought of thine heart may be forgiven thee." Acts 8:18-22

ANOINTING 101

Association brings assimilation.

"And it came to pass, when they were gone over, that Elijah said unto Elisha, Ask what I shall do for thee, before I be taken away from thee. And Elisha said, I pray thee, let a double portion of thy spirit be upon me. And he said, Thou hast asked a hard thing: nevertheless, if thou see me when I am taken from thee, it shall be so unto thee; but if not, it shall not be so."
2 Kings 2:9-10

Learn to yield to the Holy Spirit.

"If we live in the Spirit, let us also walk in the Spirit." Galatians 5:25

… **ANOINTING 101**

Fellowship with the Holy Spirit.

"The grace of the Lord Jesus Christ, and the love of God, and the communion of the Holy Ghost, be with you all. Amen."
2 Corinthians 13:14

Walking in boldness releases the anointing.

"Now when they saw the boldness of Peter and John, and perceived that they were unlearned and ignorant men, they marvelled; and they took knowledge of them, that they had been with Jesus." Acts 4:13

- **Boldness is the language satan understands**

- **Boldness is required to humiliate sickness and disease**
- **It is noticeable**
- **It is no respecter of persons**
- **It is obtained by Christ's presence.**

ANOINTING 101

RESULT

ANOINTING 101

You require it for sustenance, growth, performance and success.

"And I have filled him with the spirit of God, in wisdom, and in understanding, and in knowledge, and in all manner of workmanship, To devise cunning works, to work in gold, and in silver, and in brass, And in cutting of stones, to set them, and in carving of timber, to work in all manner of workmanship." Exodus 31:3-5

ANOINTING 101

The level of anointing determines the level of breakthrough.

"Thou preparest a table before me in the presence of mine enemies: thou anointest my head with oil; my cup runneth over." Psalm 23:5

ANOINTING 101

You cannot store it up, you have to use it and seek for more.

"But the manifestation of the Spirit is given to every man to profit withal."
1 Corinthians 12: 7

Reigning in life over situations.

The Spirit of the Lord GOD is upon me; because the LORD hath anointed me to preach good tidings unto the meek; he hath sent me to bind up the brokenhearted, to proclaim liberty to the captives, and the opening of the prison to them that are bound; To proclaim the acceptable year of the LORD, and the day of vengeance of our God; to comfort all that mourn;To appoint unto them that mourn in Zion, to give unto them beauty for ashes, the oil of joy for mourning, the garment of praise for the spirit of heaviness; that they might be called trees of righteousness, the planting of the LORD, that he might be glorified. Isaiah 61: 1-3

ANOINTING 101

You get Anointed.

"And Samuel grew, and the LORD was with him, and did let none of his words fall to the ground." 1 Samuel 3:19

- **Through Personal Contact**

- **Master Servant Relationship**

ANOINTING 101

▸ The laying on of hands

"And the LORD came down in a cloud, and spake unto him, and took of the spirit that was upon him, and gave it unto the seventy elders: and it came to pass, that, when the spirit rested upon them, they prophesied, and did not cease." Numbers 11:25

▸ The anointing oil

"And it shall come to pass in that day, that his burden shall be taken away from off thy shoulder, and his yoke from off thy neck, and the yoke shall be destroyed because of the anointing." Isaiah 10:27

The anointing will destroy what has been taking your joy away.

"To appoint unto them that mourn in Zion, to give unto them beauty for ashes, the oil of joy for mourning, the garment of praise for the spirit of heaviness; that they might be called trees of righteousness, the planting of the LORD, that he might be glorified." Isaiah 61:3

ANOINTING 101

Healing for Broken Hearted people.

"The Spirit of the Lord GOD is upon me; because the LORD hath anointed me to preach good tidings unto the meek; he hath sent me to bind up the brokenhearted, to proclaim liberty to the captives, and the opening of the prison to them that are bound." Isaiah 61:1

ANOINTING 101

When you are anointed the enemy cannot touch you.

"He suffered no man to do them wrong: yea, he reproved kings for their sakes; Saying, Touch not mine anointed, and do my prophets no harm."
Psalm 105:14-15

ANOINTING 101

The anointing in ministry is the key to exposition, provision and protection.

"Then Samuel took a vial of oil, and poured it upon his head, and kissed him, and said, Is it not because the LORD hath anointed thee to be captain over his inheritance?"

"And the Spirit of the LORD will come upon thee, and thou shalt prophesy with them, and shalt be turned into another man. And let it be, when these signs are come unto thee, that thou do as occasion serve thee; for God is with thee." 1 Samuel 10:1, 6-7

ANOINTING 101

It opens doors and tears the bars built by the enemy.

"Thus saith the LORD to his anointed, to Cyrus, whose right hand I have holden, to subdue nations before him; and I will loose the loins of kings, to open before him the two leaved gates; and the gates shall not be shut; I will go before thee, and make the crooked places straight: I will break in pieces the gates of brass, and cut in sunder the bars of iron: And I will give thee the treasures of darkness, and hidden riches of secret places, that thou mayest know that I, the LORD, which call thee by thy name, am the God of Israel." Isaiah 45:1-3

ANOINTING 101

The anointing enables.

"And I thank Christ Jesus our Lord, who hath enabled me, for that he counted me faithful, putting me into the ministry." 1 Timothy 1: 12

The anointing sets apart for service.

"And he that is the high priest among his brethren, upon whose head the anointing oil was poured, and that is consecrated to put on the garments, shall not uncover his head, nor rend his clothes; Neither shall he go in to any dead body, nor defile himself for his father, or for his mother; Neither shall he go out of the sanctuary, nor profane the sanctuary of his God; for the crown of the anointing oil of his God is upon him: I am the LORD."
Leviticus 21:10-12

Separates us from other men for God.

"As they ministered to the Lord, and fasted, the Holy Ghost said, Separate me Barnabas and Saul for the work whereunto I have called them. And when they had fasted and prayed, and laid their hands on them, they sent them away." Acts 13:2-3

He teaches all things.

> **If we allow him, we will not be swayed by every wrong doctrine.**

"Howbeit when he, the Spirit of truth, is come, he will guide you into all truth: for he shall not speak of himself; but whatsoever he shall hear, that shall he speak: and he will shew you things to come." John 16:13

ANOINTING 101

It is the key to biblical revelation.

"But the anointing which ye have received of him abideth in you, and ye need not that any man teach you: but as the same anointing teacheth you of all things, and is truth, and is no lie, and even as it hath taught you, ye shall abide in him." 1 John 2:27

ANOINTING 101

The Anointing will bring wholeness in all areas.

"And there shall come forth a rod out of the stem of Jesse, and a Branch shall grow out of his roots:

And the spirit of the LORD shall rest upon him, the spirit of wisdom and understanding, the spirit of counsel and might, the spirit of knowledge and of the fear of the LORD;"

ANOINTING 101

The anointing is the key to the deep mysteries hidden in scriptures.

"Howbeit when he, the Spirit of truth, is come, he will guide you into all truth: for he shall not speak of himself; but whatsoever he shall hear, that shall he speak: and he will shew you things to come"

"All things that the Father hath are mine: therefore said I, that he shall take of mine, and shall shew it unto you." John 16:13,15

He will transform the anointing into the umbrella of Protection.

"I will say of the LORD, He is my refuge and my fortress: my God; in him will I trust." Psalm 91: 2

Because thou hast made the LORD, which is my refuge, even the most High, thy habitation; 91:10 There shall no evil befall thee, neither shall any plague come nigh thy dwelling." Psalm 91: 9-10

ANOINTING 101

It will confirm the calling of God on your life.

"But ye shall receive power, after that the Holy Ghost is come upon you: and ye shall be witnesses unto me both in Jerusalem, and in all Judaea, and in Samaria, and unto the uttermost part of the earth." Acts 1:8

ANOINTING 101

The more the anointing you have, the more you should desire the holiness of God.

"Lord, who shall abide in thy tabernacle? who shall dwell in thy holy hill?

He that walketh uprightly, and worketh righteousness, and speaketh the truth in his heart." Psalm 15:1-2

ANOINTING 101

KEEPING IT

If you recognise your inadequacy without the Holy Spirit, He will not leave you.

"It is the spirit that quickeneth; the flesh profiteth nothing: the words that I speak unto you, they are spirit, and they are life." John 6:63

"Cast me not away from thy presence; and take not thy Holy Spirit from me." Psalm 51: 11

ANOINTING 101

Total power is accessed by total submission in the kingdom of God.

"Submit yourselves therefore to God. Resist the devil, and he will flee from you." James 4: 7

ANOINTING 101

Acknowledge the fact that holiness precedes the anointing.

"Let thy garments be always white; and let thy head lack no ointment."
Ecclesiastes 9:8

ANOINTING 101

If you walk in sin you will brake the circuit of the power of the Holy Spirit.

"And grieve not the holy Spirit of God, whereby ye are sealed unto the day of redemption." Ephesians 4: 30

You will flow in God's power as you learn the importance of total dependence.

"Now when they saw the boldness of Peter and John, and perceived that they were unlearned and ignorant men, they marvelled; and they took knowledge of them, that they had been with Jesus. And beholding the man which was healed standing with them, they could say nothing against it."
Acts 4:13-14

ANOINTING 101

Keeping the anointing is only as possible as you keep the posture of prayer.

"But ye, beloved, building up yourselves on your most holy faith, praying in the Holy Ghost." Jude 20

ANOINTING 101

Recognise the measure of grace given to you, and stay under it - when you stay within your calling, God confirms it.

"And with great power gave the apostles witness of the resurrection of the Lord Jesus: and great grace was upon them all." Acts 4:33

ANOINTING 101

The anointing that abides is the one that gives believers an inner witness about the things of God.

"But ye have an unction from the Holy One, and ye know all things."
1 John 2:20

"For as many as are led by the Spirit of God, they are the sons of God."
Romans 8:14

ANOINTING 101

The anointing helps to sanctify your heart and develop the life of Jesus in you.

"But sanctify the Lord God in your hearts: and be ready always to give an answer to every man that asketh you a reason of the hope that is in you with meekness and fear." 1 Peter 3: 15

ANOINTING 101

Know that satan respects the anointing when he sees it.

"And the man in whom the evil spirit was leaped on them, and overcame them, and prevailed against them, so that they fled out of that house naked and wounded." Acts 19:16

ANOINTING 101

CARRYING THE ANOINTING

You need to show the demons holding people in bondage that you mean business.

"The same followed Paul and us, and cried, saying, These men are the servants of the most high God, which shew unto us the way of salvation. And this did she many days. But Paul, being grieved, turned and said to the spirit, I command thee in the name of Jesus Christ to come out of her. And he came out the same hour." Acts 16: 17-18

ANOINTING 101

Watch out against the spirit of pride, Unbelief and bitterness.

"I therefore, the prisoner of the Lord, beseech you that ye walk worthy of the vocation wherewith ye are called," Ephesians 4:1

"Let all bitterness, and wrath, and anger, and clamor, and evil speaking, be put away from you, with all malice:" Ephesians 4:31

It is imperative that you will know a degree of rejection from people because of the anointing.

"But when the Philistines heard that they had anointed David king over Israel, all the Philistines came up to seek David; and David heard of it, and went down to the hold." II Samuel 5:17

ANOINTING 101

Before exaltation, is humility. Self-abnegation is the doorway to divine promotion.

"Humble yourselves therefore under the mighty hand of God, that he may exalt you in due time." 1 Peter 5:6

ANOINTING 101

There is the anointing for specific times, you can also desire the one that perpetually works through you.

"And thou shalt anoint them, as thou didst anoint their father, that they may minister unto me in the priest's office: for their anointing shall surely be an everlasting priesthood throughout their generations." Exodus 40: 15

ANOINTING 101

Refusing to let go of those who offended you can block your anointing.

"But if ye forgive not men their trespasses, neither will your Father forgive your trespasses." Matthew 6:15

ANOINTING 101

Offences are stumbling blocks. There are things you can not do anymore.

"And when ye stand praying, forgive, if ye have ought against any: that your Father also which is in heaven may forgive you your trespasses."
Mark 11:25

Water levels are used to describe the experience with the anointing.

▶ **Water**

"Jesus answered, Verily, verily, I say unto thee, Except a man be born of water and of the Spirit, he cannot enter into the kingdom of God."
John 3:5

▶ Well

"But whosoever drinketh of the water that I shall give him shall never thirst; but the water that I shall give him shall be in him a well of water springing up into everlasting life." John 4:14

▶ River

"He that believeth on me, as the scripture hath said, out of his belly shall flow rivers of living water." John 7:38

ANOINTING 101

When the Anointng flows, blessings follow.

"And be not drunk with wine, wherein is excess; but be filled with the Spirit." Ephesians 5:18

ANOINTING 101

FRIENDSHIP WITH THE HOLY SPIRIT

ANOINTING 101

Friendship with the Holy Spirit exposes you to the One who has power to act fully on behalf of Jesus.

"Peace I leave with you, my peace I give unto you: not as the world giveth, give I unto you. Let not your heart be troubled, neither let it be afraid."
John 14: 27

ANOINTING 101

He is here to remind you of all things, secular or spiritual, intended for your well-being.

"But the Comforter, which is the Holy Ghost, whom the Father will send in my name, he shall teach you all things, and bring all thingsto your remembrance, whatsoever I have said unto you." John 14: 26

ANOINTING 101

A true understanding of Jesus is only possible as you befriend the Holy Spirit.

"Nevertheless I tell you the truth; It is expedient for you that I go away: for if I go not away, the Comforter will not come unto you; but if I depart, I will send him unto you." John 16: 7

ANOINTING 101

The Holy Spirit will befriend you and continue to remind you of your right standing in God.

"And when he is come, he will reprove the world of sin, and of righteousness, and of judgment." John 16: 8

ANOINTING 101

Your friend is the embodiment of truth, when He leads you - you will not fall into error.

"Howbeit when he, the Spirit of truth, is come, he will guide youinto all truth: for he shall not speak of himself; but whatsoever heshall hear, that shall he speak: and he will shew you things to come." John 16: 13

ANOINTING 101

Friendship and intimacy with the Holy Spirit makes you desire only what please Him.

"For they that are after the flesh do mind the things of the flesh; but they that are after the Spirit the things of the Spirit." Romans 8: 5

ANOINTING 101

Intimacy with the Holy Spirit will mean starvation for your carnal nature.

"For if ye live after the flesh, ye shall die: but if ye through the Spirit do mortify the deeds of the body, ye shall live." Romans 8: 13

ANOINTING 101

Friendship with the Holy Spirit guarantees the presence of His "Fruitful qualities".

"But the fruit of the Spirit is love, joy, peace, longsuffering, gentleness, goodness, faith, meekness, temperance: against such there is no law."
Galatians 5: 22-23

ANOINTING 101

Friendship with the Holy Spirit gives you access to the wonder working power of the Holy Spirit.

"To another faith by the same Spirit; to another the gifts of healing by the same Spirit. 1 Corinthians 12: 9

ANOINTING 101